THE
SHUT-EYE
TRAIN

Eugene Field's

THE
SHUT-EYE
TRAIN

and other
Poems of Childhood
including
"Wynken, Blynken
and Nod"

Pictures by
Julia Noonan

Silver Press

For my parents on their
50th Anniversary
—J.N.

With personal thanks to Leslie Bauman and
Anna Todaro.—J.N.

Copyright © 1991 Silver Burdett Press, Inc.
Illustrations copyright © 1991 Julia Noonan
Design and art direction by Leslie Bauman
Introductory material compiled and selected by
Susan Cornell Poskanzer.
Photograph on page vii from
"Eugene Field," Charles Scribner's Sons, 1901

Published by Silver Press,
a division of Silver Burdett Press, Inc.,
Simon & Schuster, Inc. Prentice Hall Bldg.,
Englewood Cliffs, NJ 07632
For information address: Silver Press.

Printed in the United States of America
10 9 8 7 6 5 4 3 2 1

Library of Congress Cataloging-in-Publication Data

Field, Eugene, 1850-1895
The shut-eye train, and other poems of childhood /
pictures by Julia Noonan ; poems by Eugene Field. p.   cm.
Summary: A collection of poems for and about children,
many suitable for bedtime reading,
including such classics as "The Duel," "Little Boy Blue,"
and "Wynken, Blynken, and Nod."
1. Children's poetry, American. [1. American poetry.]
I. Noonan, Julia, ill.   II. Title. PS1666.N66
1991   811′.4—dc20   90-47198   CIP   AC
ISBN 0-671-73222-6 (LSB)
—ISBN 0-671-73223-4

Contents

Eugene Field
(1850–1895)

WHEN he was young, Eugene Field had no idea he'd be a poet when he grew up. His father, Roswell, had been a brilliant student who decided very early to be a lawyer. Roswell Field graduated college when he was only fifteen. He became a lawyer at seventeen, and later researched the famous Dred Scott case for the Supreme Court. Eugene Field was not the same kind of student.

According to his teacher, Eugene was "an average boy…who did not care very much for his books or his lessons." His teacher added that Eugene was very bright, but babyish, poor in math, and often sick.

Eugene's mother died when he was six. Soon after, he and his brother were sent from Missouri to Massachusetts to live with their aunt and cousin.

Even when small, Eugene enjoyed the sounds of words. He named the family's chickens Finniken, Minniken, Winniken, Dump, Poog, and Boog and he trained each one to come when called.

When he was eighteen, Eugene went to Williams College, but after eight months was asked to leave. In the next two years Eugene tried Knox College in Illinois and the University of Missouri. But he never graduated. Eugene spent too much time playing jokes and not enough on his school work. He especially enjoyed writing poems that made fun of his teachers.

Next Eugene became an actor. He formed a theater company with a friend and began writing plays for the tiny troupe. Though Eugene had a smooth bass voice, he took the parts of the women in the plays. The company failed.

Eugene's father had died while he was in college and he'd inherited $8000 in cash—a lot of money at the time. He used the entire sum to tour Europe with a friend.

When he returned, Field married his friend's sister, and decided it was time to get a real job. In his acting days, he'd met many reporters and thought he'd enjoy newspaper work. Eugene got a job at the "St. Louis Evening Journal," then later worked for other newspapers in Kansas City and Denver. From the beginning, he did little regular reporting. Instead he wrote poems and stories about interesting events and people. By 1883 his clever columns were so popular that he was asked to join a large Chicago newspaper. He stayed there, writing his column called "Sharps and Flats," for the rest of his career.

Eugene Field was a man who knew his strengths and weaknesses. He asked the newspaper to pay his salary directly to his wife. This was because he knew she was better with money. Also, he was afraid he'd spend too much on his hobbies—collecting old books, pewter cups, and antique china.

Even as an adult, Field never gave up his boyish pranks. In his newspaper offices he had a guest chair frame with no seat and was a frequent flyer of paper airplanes.

Field often struggled with his stories, writing them over and over before he was satisfied. But work on his poems was very different. They were usually published exactly as he had written them out the first time. He began to fill his columns with more poetry and in July, 1889 the newspaper published twenty-five poems in one week. He called this his "Golden Week." Thousands of fan letters poured into the newspaper.

Field, his wife, and their four children took a European trip in 1889. While at school in Germany, their oldest son died. Field wrote about his child's death in many poems. The couple later had two more children.

Eugene Field was never strong and his health grew worse in his forties. To protect his family from money worries, he quickly published five books of work taken mostly from his columns. This was both caring and wise, for one night when he was 45, Field had a heart attack and died in his sleep. Two of the last books he published were called *Trumpet and Drum* and *Love Songs of Childhood*. The poems in *The Shut-Eye Train* come from these books.

Note to Children

Take a minute. Flip through this book before you start to read it. You'll find some surprises. You'll see words that look strangely old-fashioned. You'll see others that are misspelled. You may ask: "What's going on here? And why do these poems seem 100-years old?" These are good questions.

Eugene Field enjoyed hearing the different ways people talk in different parts of the country and imitated them in his poems. If Field thought it would help you 'hear' these sounds better by writing "wuz" instead of "was," he did. Since Field studied Old English, he sometimes used words in that language too. He also enjoyed making up words that are fun to say. Try saying "Shuffle-Shoon," "rattletybang," and "amfalula" just to warm up. Knowing these secrets, will help you read the poems.

The reason some poems seem 100-years old is that they are! Today they sound like songs from another time. They tell both funny and sad stories and let us peek at life in the 1800s.

Most of the poems in *The Shut-Eye Train* are lullabies. Maybe they will help take you to sleep. You may not wear a sleeping cap as children did in Field's time. But you can still pretend to travel over hills and valleys and through star-filled skies to a place filled with sweet dreams. Close your eyes. Listen to the rhythms. Ride *The Shut-Eye Train*.

Note to Parents

In the early 1900s, just about everyone knew the name Eugene Field. He was popular nation-wide as "the poet of childhood." Parents and children read his work together. Students memorized his verses in schools and libraries bearing his name. Communities across the country celebrated "Eugene Field Day," and readings of his poems took place at Carnegie Hall in New York. The cities of Chicago and Denver erected statues in his honor. Eugene Field was a national star.

Today Field is less well-known. One reason is that he peppered his work with fairy tale terms, made-up words, Old English, and regional dialects…all ingredients that require more work of today's readers. However, it isn't necessary to "translate" every word to understand a poem. Field's bright rhythms often carry the text and the expressive pictures of *The Shut-Eye Train* lend added meaning. But those who are more curious about words and phrases may want to check the glossary on page 51.

Field's poems are more than lullabies. Gently, they push us back in our seats and open our minds to imagine all the "wonderful sights that be." This is the real magic of Eugene Field.

THE SHUT-EYE TRAIN

COME, my little one, with me!
   There are wondrous sights to see
   As the evening shadows fall;
In your pretty cap and gown,
   Don't detain
   The Shut-Eye train —
"Ting-a-ling!" the bell it goeth,
"Toot-toot!" the whistle bloweth,
And we hear the warning call:
"All aboard for Shut-Eye Town!"

Over hill and over plain
Soon will speed the Shut-Eye train!
   Through the blue where bloom the stars
   And the Mother Moon looks down
     We'll away
     To land of Fay —
   Oh, the sights that we shall see there!
   Come, my little one, with me there —
'T is a goodly train of cars —
All aboard for Shut-Eye Town!

Swifter than a wild bird's flight,
Through the realms of fleecy light
   We shall speed and speed away!
   Let the Night in envy frown —

What care we
How wroth she be!
To the Balow-land above us,
To the Balow-folk who love us,
Let us hasten while we may—
All aboard for Shut-Eye Town!

Shut-Eye Town is passing fair—
Golden dreams await us there;
We shall dream those dreams, my dear,
Till the Mother Moon goes down—
See unfold
Delights untold!
And in those mysterious places
We shall see beloved faces
And beloved voices hear
In the grace of Shut-Eye Town!

Heavy are your eyes, my sweet,
Weary are your little feet—
Nestle closer up to me
In your pretty cap and gown;
Don't detain
The Shut-Eye train!
"Ting-a-ling!" the bell it goeth,
"Toot-toot!" the whistle bloweth,
Oh, the sights that we shall see!
All aboard for Shut-Eye Town!

WYNKEN, BLYNKEN, AND NOD

WYNKEN, Blynken, and Nod one night
    Sailed off in a wooden shoe—
    Sailed on a river of crystal light,
    Into a sea of dew.
"Where are you going, and what do you wish?"
    The old moon asked the three.
"We have come to fish for the herring fish
    That live in this beautiful sea;
    Nets of silver and gold have we!"
             Said Wynken,
             Blynken,
             And Nod.

The old moon laughed and sang a song,
    As they rocked in the wooden shoe,
And the wind that sped them all night long
    Ruffled the waves of dew.
The little stars were the herring fish
    That lived in that beautiful sea—
"Now cast your nets wherever you wish—
    Never afeard are we;"
    So cried the stars to the fishermen three:
             Wynken,
             Blynken,
             And Nod.

All night long their nets they threw
    To the stars in the twinkling foam —
Then down from the skies came the wooden shoe,
    Bringing the fishermen home;
'T was all so pretty a sail it seemed
    As if it could not be,
And some folks thought 't was a dream they'd dreamed
    Of sailing that beautiful sea —
    But I shall name you the fishermen three:
            Wynken,
            Blynken,
            And Nod.

Wynken and Blynken are two little eyes,
    And Nod is a little head,
And the wooden shoe that sailed the skies
    Is a wee one's trundle-bed.
So shut your eyes while mother sings
    Of wonderful sights that be,
And you shall see the beautiful things
    As you rock the misty sea,
    Where the old shoe rocked the fishermen three:
            Wynken,
            Blynken,
            And Nod.

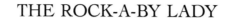

THE ROCK-A-BY LADY

THE Rock-a-By Lady from Hushaby street
    Comes stealing; comes creeping;
      The poppies they hang from her head to her feet,
And each hath a dream that is tiny and fleet—
She bringeth her poppies to you, my sweet,
    When she findeth you sleeping!

There is one little dream of a beautiful drum—
    "Rub-a-dub!" it goeth;
There is one little dream of a big sugar-plum,
And lo! thick and fast the other dreams come
Of popguns that bang, and tin tops that hum,
    And a trumpet that bloweth!

And dollies peep out of those wee little dreams
    With laughter and singing;
And boats go a-floating on silvery streams,
And the stars peek-a-boo with their own misty gleams,
And up, up, and up, where the Mother Moon beams,
    The fairies go winging!
Would you dream all these dreams that are tiny and fleet?
    They'll come to you sleeping;
So shut the two eyes that are weary, my sweet,
For the Rock-a-By Lady from Hushaby street,
With poppies that hang from her head to her feet,
    Comes stealing; comes creeping.

CHILD AND MOTHER

O MOTHER-MY-LOVE, if you'll give
    me your hand,
    And go where I ask you to wander,
I will lead you away to a beautiful land—
    The Dreamland that's waiting out yonder.
We'll walk in a sweet-posie garden out there
    Where moonlight and starlight are streaming
And the flowers and the birds are filling the air
    With the fragrance and music of dreaming.

There'll be no little tired-out boy to undress,
    No questions or cares to perplex you;
There'll be no little bruises or bumps to caress,
    Nor patching of stockings to vex you.
For I'll rock you away on a silver-dew stream,
    And sing you asleep when you're weary,
And no one shall know of our beautiful dream
    But you and your own little dearie.

And when I am tired I'll nestle my head
    In the bosom that's soothed me so often,
And the wide-awake stars shall sing in my stead
    A song which our dreaming shall soften.
So Mother-My-Love, let me take your dear hand,
    And away through the starlight we'll wander—
Away through the mist to the beautiful land—
    The Dreamland that's waiting out yonder!

THE SUGAR-PLUM TREE

HAVE you ever heard of the Sugar-Plum Tree?
  'T is a marvel of great renown!
  It blooms on the shore of the Lollipop sea
In the garden of Shut-Eye Town;
The fruit that it bears is so wondrously sweet
  (As those who have tasted it say)
That good little children have only to eat
  Of that fruit to be happy next day.

When you've got to the tree, you would have a hard time
  To capture the fruit which I sing;
The tree is so tall that no person could climb
  To the boughs where the sugar-plums swing!
But up in that tree sits a chocolate cat,
  And a gingerbread dog prowls below—
And this is the way you contrive to get at
  Those sugar-plums tempting you so:

You say but the word to that gingerbread dog
    And he barks with such terrible zest
That the chocolate cat is at once all agog,
    As her swelling proportions attest.
And the chocolate cat goes cavorting around
    From this leafy limb unto that,
And the sugar-plums tumble, of course, to the ground—
    Hurrah for that chocolate cat!

There are marshmallows, gumdrops, and peppermint canes,
    With stripings of scarlet or gold,
And you carry away of the treasure that rains
    As much as your apron can hold!
So come, little child, cuddle closer to me
    In your dainty white nightcap and gown,
And I'll rock you away to that Sugar-Plum Tree
    In the garden of Shut-Eye Town.

18

THE NIGHT WIND

HAVE you ever heard the wind go "Yooooo"?
      'T is a pitiful sound to hear!
      It seems to chill you through and through
   With a strange and speechless fear.
'T is the voice of the night that broods outside
   When folk should be asleep,
And many and many's the time I've cried
To the darkness brooding far and wide
   Over the land and the deep:
   "Whom do you want, O lonely night,
      That you wail the long hours through?"
And the night would say in its ghostly way:
            "Yooooooooo!
            Yooooooooo!
            Yooooooooo!"

19

My mother told me long ago
   (When I was a little tad)
That when the night went wailing so,
   Somebody had been bad;
And then, when I was snug in bed,
   Whither I had been sent,
With the blankets pulled up round my head,
I'd think of what my mother'd said,
   And wonder what boy she meant!
And "Who's been bad to-day?" I'd ask
   Of the wind that hoarsely blew,
And the voice would say in its meaningful way:
         "Yooooooooo!
          Yoooooooo!
          Yooooooooo!"

That this was true I must allow—
   You'll not believe it, though!
Yes, though I'm quite a model now,
   I was not always so.
And if you doubt what things I say,
   Suppose you make the test;
Suppose, when you've been bad some day
And up to bed are sent away
   From mother and the rest—
Suppose you ask, "Who has been bad?"
   And then you'll hear what's true;
For the wind will moan in its ruefulest tone:
         "Yooooooooo!
          Yoooooooo!
          Yooooooooo!"

SEEIN' THINGS

I AIN'T afeard uv snakes, or toads, or bugs, or worms,
   or mice,
   An' things 'at girls are skeered uv I think are
      awful nice!
I'm pretty brave, I guess; an' yet I hate to go to bed,
For, when I'm tucked up warm an' snug an' when my
   prayers are said,
Mother tells me "Happy dreams!" and takes away the light,
An' leaves me lyin' all alone an' seein' things at night!

Sometimes they're in the corner, sometimes they're by the
    door,
Sometimes they're all a-standin' in the middle uv the floor;
Sometimes they are a-sittin' down, sometimes they're walkin'
    round
So softly an' so creepylike they never make a sound!
Sometimes they are as black as ink, an' other times they're
    white—
But the color ain't no difference when you see things at night!

Once, when I licked a feller 'at had just moved on our street,
An' father sent me up to bed without a bite to eat,
I woke up in the dark an' saw things standin' in a row,
A-lookin' at me cross-eyed an' p'intin' at me—so!
Oh, my! I wuz so skeered that time I never slep' a mite—
It's almost alluz when I'm bad I see things at night!

Lucky thing I ain't a girl, or I'd be skeered to death!
Bein' I'm a boy, I duck my head an' hold my breath;
An' I am, oh! *so* sorry I'm a naughty boy, an' then
I promise to be better an' I say my prayers again!
Gran'ma tells me that's the only way to make it right
When a feller has been wicked an' sees things at night!

An' so, when other naughty boys would coax me into sin,
I try to skwush the Tempter's voice 'at urges me within;
An' when they's pie for supper, or cakes 'at's big an' nice,
I want to—but I do not pass my plate f'r them things twice!
No, ruther let Starvation wipe me slowly out o' sight
Than I should keep a-livin' on an' seein' things at night!

23

THE DINKEY-BIRD

IN an ocean, 'way out yonder
    (As all sapient people know),
  Is the land of Wonder-Wander,
Whither children love to go;
It's their playing, romping, swinging,
  That give great joy to me
While the Dinkey-Bird goes singing
  In the amfalula tree!

There the gum-drops grow like cherries,
  And taffy's thick as peas—
Caramels you pick like berries
  When, and where, and how you please;
Big red sugar-plums are clinging
  To the cliffs beside that sea
Where the Dinkey-Bird is singing
  In the amfalula tree.

So when children shout and scamper
  And make merry all the day,
When there's naught to put a damper
  To the ardor of their play;
When I hear their laughter ringing,
  Then I'm sure as sure can be
That the Dinkey-Bird is singing
  In the amfalula tree.

For the Dinkey-Bird's bravuras
    And staccatos are so sweet—
His roulades, appoggiaturas,
    And robustos so complete,
That the youth of every nation—
    Be they near or far away—
Have especial delectation
    In that gladsome roundelay.

Their eyes grow bright and brighter
    Their lungs begin to crow,
Their hearts get light and lighter,
    And their cheeks are all aglow;
For an echo cometh bringing
    The news to all and me,
That the Dinkey-Bird is singing
    In the amfalula tree.

I'm sure you like to go there
    To see your feathered friend—
And so many goodies grow there
    You would like to comprehend!
Speed, little dreams, your winging
    To that land across the sea
Where the Dinkey-Bird is singing
    In the amfalula tree!

please
Come to
our party
♥♥♥ Dinkey

THE FLY-AWAY HORSE

OH, a wonderful horse is the Fly-Away Horse—
   Perhaps you have seen him before;
   Perhaps, while you slept, his shadow has swept
  Through the moonlight that floats on the floor.
For it's only at night, when the stars twinkle bright,
  That the Fly-Away Horse, with a neigh
And a pull at his rein and a toss of his mane,
  Is up on his heels and away!
     The Moon in the sky,
     As he gallopeth by,
  Cries: "Oh! what a marvellous sight!"
     And the Stars in dismay
     Hide their faces away
In the lap of old Grandmother Night.

It is yonder, out yonder, the Fly-Away Horse
     Speedeth ever and ever away—
Over meadows and lanes, over mountains and plains,
     Over streamlets that sing at their play;
And over the sea like a ghost sweepeth he,
     While the ships they go sailing below,
And he speedeth so fast that the men at the mast
     Adjudge him some portent of woe.
          "What ho there!" they cry,
               As he flourishes by
          With a whisk of his beautiful tail;
               And the fish in the sea
               Are as scared as can be,
          From the nautilus up to the whale!

31

And the Fly-Away Horse seeks those far-away lands
    You little folk dream of at night—
Where candy-trees grow, and honey-brooks flow,
    And corn-fields with popcorn are white;
And the beasts in the wood are ever so good
    To children who visit them there—
What glory astride of a lion to ride,
    Or to wrestle around with a bear!
        The monkeys, they say:
        "Come on, let us play,"
    And they frisk in the cocoanut-trees:
        While the parrots, that cling
        To the peanut-vines, sing
    Or converse with comparative ease!

Off! scamper to bed—you shall ride him to-night!
    For, as soon as you've fallen asleep,
With a jubilant neigh he shall bear you away
    Over forest and hillside and deep!
But tell us, my dear, all you see and you hear
    In those beautiful lands over there,
Where the Fly-Away Horse wings his far-away course
    With the wee one consigned to his care.
        Then grandma will cry
        In amazement: "Oh, my!"
    And she'll think it could never be so;
        And only we two
        Shall know it is true—
    You and I, little precious! shall know!

SHUFFLE-SHOON AND AMBER-LOCKS

SHUFFLE-SHOON and Amber-Locks
    Sit together, building blocks;
        Shuffle-Shoon is old and gray,
      Amber-Locks a little child,
    But together at their play
      Age and Youth are reconciled,
And with sympathetic glee
Build their castles fair to see.

  "When I grow to be a man"
(So the wee one's prattle ran),
    "I shall build a castle so—
      With a gateway broad and grand;
    Here a pretty vine shall grow,
      There a soldier guard shall stand;
And the tower shall be so high,
Folks will wonder, by and by!"

Shuffle-Shoon quoth: "Yes, I know;
Thus I builded long ago!
    Here a gate and there a wall,
      Here a window, there a door;
    Here a steeple wondrous tall
      Riseth ever more and more!
But the years have levelled low
What I builded long ago!"

  So they gossip at their play,
Heedless of the fleeting day;

One speaks of the Long Ago
    Where his dead hopes buried lie;
One with chubby cheeks aglow
    Prattleth of the By and By;
Side by side they build their blocks—
Shuffle-Shoon and Amber-Locks.

35

THE RIDE TO BUMPVILLE

PLAY that my knee was a calico mare
    Saddled and bridled for Bumpville;
      Leap to the back of this steed, if you dare,
  And gallop away to Bumpville!
I hope you'll be sure to sit fast in your seat,
For this calico mare is prodigiously fleet,
And many adventures you're likely to meet
    As you journey along to Bumpville.

This calico mare both gallops and trots
    While whisking you off to Bumpville;
She paces, she shies, and she stumbles, in spots,
    In the tortuous road to Bumpville;
And sometimes this strangely mercurial steed
Will suddenly stop and refuse to proceed,
Which, all will admit, is vexatious indeed,
    When one is en route to Bumpville!

She's scared of the cars when the engine goes "Toot!"
    Down by the crossing at Bumpville;
You'd better look out for that treacherous brute
    Bearing you off to Bumpville!
With a snort she rears up on her hindermost heels,
And executes jigs and Virginia reels—
Words fail to explain how embarrassed one feels
    Dancing so wildly to Bumpville!

It's bumpytybump and it's jiggytyjog,
    Journeying on to Bumpville;
It's over the hilltop and down through the bog
    You ride on your way to Bumpville;
It's rattletybang over boulder and stump,
There are rivers to ford, there are fences to jump,
And the corduroy road it goes bumpytybump,
    Mile after mile to Bumpville!

Perhaps you'll observe it's no easy thing
    Making the journey to Bumpville,
So I think, on the whole, it were prudent to bring
    An end to this ride to Bumpville;
For, though she has uttered no protest or plaint,
The calico mare must be blowing and faint—
What's more to the point, I'm blowed if I ain't!
    So play we have got to Bumpville!

OVER THE HILLS AND FAR AWAY

OVER the hills and far away,
　　A little boy steals from his morning play,
　　And under the blossoming apple-tree
He lies and he dreams of the things to be:
Of battles fought and of victories won,
Of wrongs o'erthrown and of great deeds done—
Of the valor that he shall prove some day,
Over the hills and far away—
　　　　Over the hills and far away!

Over the hills and far away
It's, oh, for the toil the livelong day!
But it mattereth not to the soul aflame
With a love for riches and power and fame!
On, O man! while the sun is high—
On to the certain joys that lie
Yonder where blazeth the noon of day,
Over the hills and far away—
　　　　Over the hills and far away!

Over the hills and far away,
An old man lingers at close of day;
Now that his journey is almost done,
His battles fought and his victories won—
The old-time honesty and truth,
The trustfulness and the friends of youth,
Home and mother—where are they?
Over the hills and far away—
　　　　Over the years and far away!

THE DUEL

THE gingham dog and the calico cat
  Side by side on the table sat;
   'Twas half-past twelve, and (what do
    you think!)
Nor one nor t' other had slept a wink!
  The old Dutch clock and the Chinese plate
  Appeared to know as sure as fate
There was going to be a terrible spat.
   (I wasn't there; I simply state
   What was told to me by the Chinese plate!)

The gingham dog went "bow-wow-wow!"
And the calico cat replied "mee-ow!"
The air was littered, an hour or so,
With bits of gingham and calico,
  While the old Dutch clock in the chimney-place
  Up with its hands before its face,
For it always dreaded a family row!
   (Now mind: I'm only telling you
   What the old Dutch clock declares is true!)

The Chinese plate looked very blue,
And wailed, "Oh, dear! what shall we do!"
But the gingham dog and the calico cat
Wallowed this way and tumbled that,
    Employing every tooth and claw
    In the awfullest way you ever saw—
And, oh! how the gingham and calico flew!
    (Don't fancy I exaggerate—
    I got my news from the Chinese plate!)

Next morning, where the two had sat
They found no trace of dog or cat;
And some folks think unto this day
That burglars stole that pair away!
    But the truth about the cat and pup
    Is this: they ate each other up!
Now what do you really think of that!
    (The old Dutch clock it told me so,
    And that is how I came to know.)

43

LITTLE BOY BLUE

THE little toy dog is covered with dust,
    But sturdy and staunch he stands;
    And the little toy soldier is red with rust,
And his musket moulds in his hands.
Time was when the little toy dog was new,
    And the soldier was passing fair;
And that was the time when our Little Boy Blue
    Kissed them and put them there.

"Now, don't you go till I come," he said,
    "And don't you make any noise!"
So, toddling off to his trundle-bed,
    He dreamt of the pretty toys;
And, as he was dreaming, an angel song
    Awakened our Little Boy Blue—
Oh! the years are many, the years are long,
    But the little toy friends are true!
Aye, faithful to Little Boy Blue they stand,
    Each in the same old place—
Awaiting the touch of a little hand,
    The smile of a little face;
And they wonder, as waiting the long years through
    In the dust of that little chair,
What has become of our Little Boy Blue,
    Since he kissed them and put them there.

45

PITTYPAT AND TIPPYTOE

ALL day long they come and go—
    Pittypat and Tippytoe;
        Footprints up and down the hall,
    Playthings scattered on the floor,
Finger-marks along the wall,
    Tell-tale smudges on the door—
By these presents you shall know
Pittypat and Tippytoe.

    How they riot at their play!
And a dozen times a day
    In they troop, demanding bread—
        Only buttered bread will do,
    And that butter must be spread
        Inches thick with sugar too!
And I never can say, "No,
Pittypat and Tippytoe!"

    Sometimes there are griefs to soothe,
Sometimes ruffled brows to smooth;
    For (I much regret to say)
        Tippytoe and Pittypat
    Sometimes interrupt their play
        With an internecine spat;
Fie, for shame! to quarrel so—
Pittypat and Tippytoe!

47

Oh, the thousand worrying things
Every day recurrent brings!
    Hands to scrub and hair to brush,
        Search for playthings gone amiss,
    Many a wee complaint to hush,
        Many a little bump to kiss;
Life seems one vain, fleeting show
To Pittypat and Tippytoe!

    And when day is at an end,
There are little duds to mend:
    Little frocks are strangely torn,
        Little shoes great holes reveal,
    Little hose, but one day worn,
        Rudely yawn at toe and heel!
Who but *you* could work such woe,
Pittypat and Tippytoe?

But when comes this thought to me:
"Some there are that childless be,"
    Stealing to their little beds,
        With a love I cannot speak,
    Tenderly I stroke their heads
        Fondly kiss each velvet cheek.
God help those who do not know
A Pittypat or Tippytoe!

    On the floor and down the hall,
Rudely smutched upon the wall,
    There are proofs in every kind
        Of the havoc they have wrought,
    And upon my heart you'd find
        Just such trade-marks, if you sought;
Oh, how glad I am 't is so,
Pittypat and Tippytoe!

Glossary

agog	very excited
appoggiaturas	ornamental notes that come before main notes in music
Balow-land	lullaby land
bravuras	flowery passages of music
checkerberries	red fruit of wintergreen plants
delectation	enjoyment
gladsome roundelay	happy part of a song that is repeated over and over again
internecine spat	destructive fight
Land of Fay	Fairy Land
mercurial steed	changeable, high-spirited horse
nautilus	small shellfish
pickerel	fresh-water fish
p'intin'	pointing
prodigiously fleet	wonderfully fast
robustos	songs that are sung in a powerful way
roulades	quick sequences of notes in music
ruefulest	most unhappy
sapient	wise
vexatious	annoying
wroth	angry

A NOTE FROM THE ARTIST

While working on *The Shut-Eye Train* I have had
the pleasure of bringing to life many of my own childhood
memories as well as drawing upon my feelings as a
parent. I hope that as a reader you will find a warm
familiar spot for yourself amongst what my eight year old
son calls "Mom's drawings from the dream world".
The paintings were produced on Arches hot press
paper with colored pencil drawing over an underlying
wash of alkyd paint.
It is my pleasure to offer them now to you.
Sincerely,

Julia Noonan